REVELATION

Little Rock Scripture Study Staff

LITTLE ROCK SCRIPTURE STUDY

*A ministry of the Diocese of Little Rock
in partnership with Liturgical Press*

DIOCESE OF LITTLE ROCK

2500 North Tyler Street • P.O. Box 7565 • Little Rock, Arkansas 72217 • (501) 664-0340 Fax (501) 664-6304

Office of the Bishop

Dear Friends in Christ,

Sacred Scripture is a wealth of inspired wisdom express-
ing Christian truths which challenge us to deepen our
relationship with God. Although the Bible can be intimi-
dating, it is important that we study God's word in the
Scriptures, because it is the basis of our faith and offers us
the thoughts and experiences of Christians past and
present. It is God speaking to us through the insights of
Church fathers and later saints.

I am pleased to present this study guide from Little Rock
Scripture Study to serve as an aid for reflection and con-
templation in your reading of Scripture. At the same time,
the guide will give you insight into how to apply what you
have read to your life today.

I encourage you to read Sacred Scripture slowly and
reflectively so that it can penetrate your heart and mind.
It is my hope that the Word of God will empower you as
Christians to live a life worthy of your call as a child of God
and a member of the body of Christ.

Sincerely in Christ,

✠ Anthony B. Taylor
Bishop of Little Rock

Sacred Scripture

"The Church has always venerated the divine Scriptures just as she venerates the body of the Lord, since from the table of both the word of God and of the body of Christ she unceasingly receives and offers to the faithful the bread of life, especially in the sacred liturgy. She has always regarded the Scriptures together with sacred tradition as the supreme rule of faith, and will ever do so. For, inspired by God and committed once and for all to writing, they impart the word of God Himself without change, and make the voice of the Holy Spirit resound in the words of the prophets and apostles. Therefore, like the Christian religion itself, all the preaching of the Church must be nourished and ruled by sacred Scripture. For in the sacred books, the Father who is in heaven meets His children with great love and speaks with them; and the force and power in the word of God is so great that it remains the support and energy of the Church, the strength of faith for her sons, the food of the soul, the pure and perennial source of spiritual life."

Vatican II, Dogmatic Constitution on Divine Revelation, no. 21.

INTERPRETATION OF SACRED SCRIPTURE

"Since God speaks in sacred Scripture through men in human fashion, the interpreter of sacred Scripture, in order to see clearly what God wanted to communicate to us, should carefully investigate what meaning the sacred writers really intended, and what God wanted to manifest by means of their words.

"Those who search out the intention of the sacred writers must, among other things, have regard for 'literary forms.' For truth is proposed and expressed in a variety of ways, depending on whether a text is history of one kind or another, or whether its form is that of prophecy, poetry, or some other type of speech. The interpreter must investigate what meaning the sacred writer intended to express and actually expressed in particular circumstances as he used contemporary literary forms in accordance with the situation of his own time and culture. For the correct understanding of what the sacred author wanted to assert, due attention must be paid to the customary and characteristic styles of perceiving, speaking, and narrating which prevailed at the time of the sacred writer, and to the customs men normally followed in that period in their everyday dealings with one another."

Vatican II, Dogmatic Constitution on Divine Revelation, no. 12.

Instructions

MATERIALS FOR THE STUDY

This Study Guide: Revelation

Bible: The New American Bible with Revised New Testament or The New Jerusalem Bible is recommended. Paraphrased editions are discouraged as they offer little if any help when facing difficult textual questions. Choose a Bible you feel free to write in or underline.

Commentary: The New Collegeville Bible Commentary, volume 12, *The Book of Revelation* by Catherine A. Cory (Liturgical Press) is used with this study. The abbreviation for this commentary, NCBC-NT volume 12, and the assigned pages are found at the beginning of each lesson.

ADDITIONAL MATERIALS

Bible Dictionary: *The Dictionary of the Bible* by John L. McKenzie (Simon & Schuster) is highly recommended as a reference.

Notebook: A notebook may be used for lecture notes and your personal reflections.

WEEKLY LESSONS

Lesson 1—Rev 1
Lesson 2—Rev 2–3
Lesson 3—Rev 4–7
Lesson 4—Rev 8–11

Lesson 5—Rev 12–14
Lesson 6—Rev 15–18
Lesson 7—Rev 19–22

YOUR DAILY PERSONAL STUDY

The first step is prayer. Open your heart and mind to God. Reading Scripture is an opportunity to listen to God who loves you. Pray that the same Holy Spirit who guided the formation of Scripture will inspire you to correctly understand what you read and empower you to make what you read a part of your life.

The next step is commitment. Daily spiritual food is as necessary as food for the body. This study is divided into daily units. Schedule a regular time and place for your study, as free from distractions as possible. Allow about twenty minutes a day. Make it a daily appointment with God.

As you begin each lesson read the assigned chapters of Scripture found at the beginning of each lesson, the footnotes in your Bible, and then the indicated pages of the commentary. This preparation will give you an overview of the entire lesson and help you to appreciate the context of individual passages.

As you reflect on Scripture, ask yourself these four questions:

1. *What does the Scripture passage say?*
   Read the passage slowly and reflectively. Use your imagination to picture the scene or enter into it.

2. *What does the Scripture passage mean?*
   Read the footnotes and the commentary to help you understand what the sacred writers intended and what God wanted to communicate by means of their words.

3. *What does the Scripture passage mean to me?*
   Meditate on the passage. God's Word is living and powerful. What is God saying to you today? How does the Scripture passage apply to your life today?

4. *What am I going to do about it?*
   Try to discover how God may be challenging you in this passage. An encounter with God contains a challenge to know God's will and follow it more closely in daily life.

THE QUESTIONS ASSIGNED FOR EACH DAY

Read the questions and references for each day. The questions are designed to help you listen to God's Word and to prepare you for the weekly small-group discussion.

Some of the questions can be answered briefly and objectively by referring to the Bible references and the commentary *(What does the passage say?)*. Some will lead you to a better understanding of how the Scriptures apply to the Church, sacraments, and society *(What does the passage mean?)*. Some questions will invite you to consider how God's Word challenges or supports you in your relationships with God and others *(What does the passage mean to me?)*. Finally, the questions will lead you to examine your actions in light of Scripture *(What am I going to do about it?)*.

Write your responses in this study guide or in a notebook to help you clarify and organize your thoughts and feelings.

THE WEEKLY SMALL-GROUP MEETING

The weekly small-group sharing is the heart of the Little Rock Scripture Study Program. Participants gather in small groups to share the results of praying, reading, and reflecting on Scripture and on the assigned questions. The goal of the discussion is for group members to be strengthened and nourished individually and as a community through sharing how God's Word speaks to them and affects their daily lives. The daily study questions will guide the discussion; it is not necessary to discuss all the questions.

All members share the responsibility of creating an atmosphere of loving support and trust in the group by respecting the opinions and experiences of others, and by affirming and encouraging one another. The simple shared prayer which begins and ends each small group meeting also helps create the open and trusting environment in which group members can share their faith deeply and grow in the study of God's Word.

A distinctive feature of this program is its emphasis on and trust in God's presence working in and through each member. Sharing responses to God's presence in the Word and in others can bring about remarkable growth and transformation.

THE WRAP-UP LECTURE

The lecture is designed to develop and clarify the themes of each lesson. It is not intended to be the focus of the group's discussion. For this reason, the lecture always occurs *after* the small group discussion. If several small groups meet at one time, the groups may gather in a central location to listen to the lecture.

Lectures may be presented by a local speaker. They are also available in audio form on CD and in visual form on DVD.

Revelation I

NCBC-NT VOLUME 12, PAGES 5–20

Day I

1. List some words, themes, opinions, or concerns that immediately come to mind as you begin to study the book of Revelation.

2. a) Identify three purposes of apocalyptic literature.

   b) Are these new to you?

3. How much do we know about . . .

   a) The author of the book of Revelation?

   b) The date of its completion?

   c) John's original audience?

Day 2

4. What does the word "apocalypse" mean, and what is the typical subject matter of apocalyptic visions?

5. How do we know that John's writings were meant for his contemporaries (1:1)?

6. What makes John's revelation a "prophetic" message (1:3)?

Day 3

7. Jesus is described with a series of three titles (1:5). Which is most meaningful to you personally? Why? (See 3:14; Ps 89:37-38; 1 Cor 15:20.)

8. Also in a series of three, John lists Jesus' actions on behalf of the people.

   a) What does John say that would console his readers?

   b) When you consider what Jesus has done in your life, what comes to mind first?

Day 4

9. a) Discuss the significance that verse 9 would have had for John's readers.

    b) What is the significance of the words "distress," "kingdom," and "endurance" (1:9)?

10. Why does John address the particular churches listed in 1:11? Why only seven?

11. "One like the son of man . . ." (1:13) symbolizes God in the midst of his people. Where else in the Old Testament do we find similar symbolic images of God's presence? (See Exod 13:21-22; 19:16-20; Ps 139:7-12; Dan 7:13-14; 10:5-6.)

Day 5

12. Why does John talk about the eyes, hands, and feet of the figure in his vision (1:14-15)?

13. The image of Jesus in 1:13-16 appeals to the senses and to the imagination. What image of Jesus captures your imagination? Why? (See Matt 3:12; 11:28-30; 23:37; Luke 12:49-53; 19:32-38; John 1:14; 6:18-21, 48-51; 8:12; 10:7-15.)

14. a) What does a two-edged sword symbolize in apocalyptic literature (1:16)?

    b) When has the Word of God been a two-edged sword for you?

Day 6

15. a) How would the words of Jesus in verses 17 and 18 give hope to persecuted Christians?

    b) Recall a time when you needed to be reassured that Jesus remains in the world.

16. What do the seven stars represent (1:20)?

17. Recall things from this week's study that surprised you, as well as those that confirmed your previous understanding of Revelation.

Revelation 2–3

NCBC-NT VOLUME 12, PAGES 20–31

Day 1

1. What did you learn last week that may help you through the entire study of Revelation?

2. From your commentary reading, find as many reasons as you can to explain why the church at Ephesus is the first church John addresses.

3. a) List the positive qualities John finds in the Ephesian Christian community (2:2-3).

   b) Which of these qualities could be applied to your parish? Give an example.

Day 2

4. a) What is John's accusation against the Ephesians (1:4)?

   b) What do we know about the culture that might have caused the Ephesians' shortcomings?

5. Why would Christ's promise of "the right to eat from the tree of life" be especially appealing in Ephesus (2:7)? (See Acts 19:26-27.)

6. a) How can Christians in Smyrna be both poor and rich (2:9)? (See Ps 9:19; 72:12-13; Jas 2:5.)

   b) Recall someone you know who is poor in the economic sense, and yet seems secure and at peace. What brings them security?

Day 3

7. a) What conflicts may have been going on in Smyrna (2:8-10)?

   b) In what ways do Christians face these types of conflicts today?

8. a) What problem is found both in Pergamum (2:14) and in Thyatira (2:20)?

   b) Why does John consider this a dangerous lapse among Christians?

9. If John was to write a letter to your parish community, what might he praise and how would he encourage improvement?

Day 4

10. Christ is described as the "searcher of hearts and minds" (2:23). Does this frighten or console you, or both? (See Ps 139.)

11. John appears not to be fooled by the good reputation of Sardis. How can a Christian community look good on the outside but really be "dead" (3:1)? (See Heb 3:12-14; Jas 2:14-17.)

12. What does the color white symbolize (3:4-5)? (See 2:17; 3:18; 7:13-14; 19:11-14.)

Day 5

13. a) What do the key of David and the open door represent (3:7-8)? (See also 3:20; 4:1; Acts 14:27; 1 Cor 16:9.)

    b) Name an opportunity that Christ has given you and explore how well you have taken advantage of it.

14. John used a natural phenomenon to warn against spiritual mediocrity (3:15-16). Name some of life's distractions that get in the way and make you lukewarm as a Christian.

Day 6

15. In the Old Testament "fire refined gold" symbolized the purifying effects of suffering (see Mal 3:2). Recall a time in your own life when suffering helped "purify" you or your life in some way.

16. The Laodicians' wealth led them to believe they were spiritually elite (3:17). How do you respond when you encounter this attitude?

17. Recall the three goals of apocalyptic literature. Then find in these seven letters specific messages that fulfill each purpose.

Revelation 4–7

NCBC-NT VOLUME 12, PAGES 31–41

Day 1

1. Name some similarities you discovered last week between the churches of Asia Minor and the churches of today.

2. a) When is a vision a theophany?

   b) Describe a typical Old Testament theophany. (See Exod 19:16-25.)

3. Read the prayer of the four living creatures in 4:8. How does their experience of God reflect other experiences with the divine? (See, for example, Exod 3:4-5; Ps 99; 111; Isa 6:1-8; Mark 1:23-24; Luke 1:49; Heb 7:26.)

Day 2

4. a) What titles do you find for Jesus in 5:5?

   b) Name other messianic titles found in Scripture. (See Isa 11:1-10; Matt 1:1; Mark 1:24; Rev 22:16.)

5. The title "Lamb" is used to speak of Christ (5:6, 12, 13). How had the Lamb become worthy to open the scroll (5:5-10)?

6. How would the liturgy or prayer scene have brought comfort to John's readers (5:8-14)?

Day 3

7. a) What powers are the four horsemen given (6:1-7)?

   b) Which do you think represents the greatest threat to the world today? Give examples.

8. Scarcity, death, displacement, maiming, all are consequences of warfare (6:3-11). What are your experiences with these, or other lesser-known costs of war or civil conflict?

9. In what ways are you able to bear witness to the Word of God (6:9)? (See Rom 10:13-15; 2 Cor 5:20; Jas 1:19-27.)

Matthew angel – Jesus
in Carnation
& human nature

Luke - ox - sacrifice

John - eagle - soars -
closer to divine

Mark - lion - courage

Day 4

10. a) What cosmic signs do we find in 6:12-14 and how do the people respond to them?

    b) What sign of hope can be found in these typical apocalyptic signs? (See Matt 24:29-31; Mark 13:3-8.)

11. In what way and how soon does the mood shift after chapter 6? (See 7:1.)

Day 5

12. What difference does it make to be "sealed as a servant of God" (7:3)? (See 14:1; 2 Cor 1:21-22; Eph 1:13-14; 4:30.)

13. Name some of the ancient events associated with being sealed (7:3). (See Gen 4:13-15; Exod 12:7-14; Ezek 9:4-6.)

14. a) Would John's readers have taken the number 144,000 literally (7:4)?

    b) Why is that important for us to know?

Day 6

15. What do white robes and palm branches symbolize (7:9)? (See 1 Macc 13:51; 2 Macc 10:7.)

16. Describe the connection between forgiveness and the blood of the Lamb (7:14). (See Isa 1:18; Heb 9:22; 1 John 1:7.)

17. Read 7:13-17. Take some time to imagine yourself in this ancient liturgy and meditate on the scene. Pay attention to your emotional reactions, the way you envision God and God's throne, the people you see standing before the throne, etc. Then respond to the reading in any way you can.

Revelation 8–11

NCBC-NT VOLUME 12, PAGES 41–52

Day 1

1. What feelings did you experience when studying the scroll and seven seals in last week's lesson?

2. John uses silence for dramatic effect (8:1). When has silence been especially important in your prayer life? Why?

3. a) How do the plagues in Egypt compare with the first four trumpet blasts (8:6-12)? (See Exod 7:20; 9:23-26; 10:21-23.)

   b) How can the "plagues" released by the trumpets be considered miracles?

Day 2

4. What does one-third symbolize and what message does it send (8:7, 9-12)?

5. Compare the description of the locusts (9:7-11) with the imagery in 6:1-2. What significant imagery do these two readings share?

6. As you read chapter 9, the situation seems desperate. Explain how the use of passive verbs signifies hope and consolation (9:1, 3, 5).

Day 3

7. List attitudes, beliefs, and behaviors that show others that you are among those "sealed" (9:4). (See Eph 1:13-14.)

8. If we took John's words about the locusts literally, how would we miss the "truth" of his message (9:3-10)?

9. We read that one-third of the population was destroyed, and yet the survivors still did not repent (9:18, 20-21). How could that be? (See Exod 9:12, 34; Isa 65:2; Acts 19:9.)

Day 4

10. Your commentary states that John's message in 9:7 is that "evil has a *human* face." Give some examples to illustrate this lesson.

11. John warns against worshiping idols made from gold, silver, bronze, etc. (9:20).

    a) Name some idols our culture worships.

    b) Are there any idols you cling to?

12. Why would the command to prophesy (10:11) have been "sour" both to John and to Ezekiel? (See Ezek 3:1-4.)

Day 5

13. a) Find the connection between the two witnesses (11:3-6) and Zechariah 4–6.

    b) What other Old Testament parallel could be drawn? (See Ezek 7:14-25; Sir 48:1; 1 Kgs 17:1.)

14. Identify the main message of the vision in 11:7-13.

Day 6

15. Why is the "great city" given the symbolic names of Sodom and Egypt (11:8)? (See Gen 18:22-32; Exod 1:11-14; Isa 1:10.)

16. a) Identify the legend about the ark of the covenant (11:19) that would have been familiar to John's readers. (See 2 Macc 2:4-8; Exod 25:10, 22.)

    b) Why does John's vision of the ark restore hope?

17. a) What motivates the people to praise God in 11:13? In 11:15-18?

    b) In your own life, what experience(s) have led you to pray most fervently?

Revelation 12–14

NCBC-NT VOLUME 12, PAGES 52–67

Day 1

1. Which part of last week's group discussion most helped you to understand the lesson?

2. Find at least three messages or symbols of hope and consolation in the vision of the woman and the dragon (12:1-6).

3. Why is the desert a symbol of comfort, especially for those being persecuted (12:6)? (See Exod 16:32; Deut 32:10; Amos 2:10; Mic 4:10.)

Day 2

4. John does not tell his readers the identity of the woman. Whom *could* she represent (12:1-6)? (See Gen 3:14-16; Isa 66:7-13; Rev 12:10-11; 12:17.)

5. What does the battle between Michael and the dragon symbolize (12:7-9)? (See Col 1:13.)

6. a) Identify the dragon's names (12:9) and whether they are fitting names for evil. (See Gen 3:12-16.)

   b) Name some ways you win against evil on a daily basis.

Day 3

7. Find clues to indicate the identity of the beast (13:1-10).

8. "Fascinated, the whole world followed after the beast" (13:3). What fascinations distract you from your commitment to Christ, especially to prayer and service? (See Col 2:8.) What happens in your life as a result?

9. What does John mean when he writes "forty-two months" (three and one-half years) (13:5)?

Day 4

10. a) Name the ways the beast from the earth (13:11-18) is related to the first beast (13:1) and to the dragon (12:3).

    b) What conclusion can we draw about the second beast's identity?

11. John uses code language to describe common Roman practices and demands made of Roman citizens. What are they (13:11-17)? (See 19:20; Matt 24:24.)

12. a) Most likely, what does the number 666 symbolize (13:18)? Why?

    b) In what ways have you heard this Scripture verse misused?

Day 5

13. John speaks of 144,000 who have not engaged in sexual activity (14:4). Discuss both the literal and the figurative meanings this passage could have.

14. Recall a time when fear of God's judgment helped you change a sinful attitude or behavior (14:7).

15. Why is Babylon associated with God's judgment (14:8)? (See 18:1-24; Isa 21:9; Jer 51.)

Day 6

16. Read the vision in 14:9-13.

    a) What symbolic imagery in this vision would have encouraged those who were loyal to God's covenant to persevere?

    b) What imagery would have encouraged the disloyal to repent?

17. How do you reconcile the picture of God's fury in 14:10-11 with more moving and protecting images of God found elsewhere in the Bible?

18. What does harvesting with the sickle represent (14:14-19)? (See 6:10; Isa 63:1-6; Joel 4:13; Matt 13:36-43.)

Revelation 15–18

NCBC-NT VOLUME 12, PAGES 67–80

Day 1

1. What was particularly challenging to you in last week's lesson?

2. Read the songs of Moses in Exodus 15:1-18 and Deuteronomy 32:3-4. How is the martyrs' song (Rev 15:2-4) similar?

3. Find the Temple images in 15:5-8. (See Exod 33:7-11.)

Day 2

4. a) What is the goal of God's fury (16:1-9)?

   b) What Exodus event is John recalling in the seven bowls image? (See Exod 7–11.)

5. a) Even when plunged into darkness the people do not repent of their "works" (16:11). What does John mean by "works"?

   b) Can you recall times in your own life that you chose to remain in "darkness"?

6. How can the image of the thief and the blessing that follows (16:15) help shape today's Christians' attitudes about God's final judgment? (See 1 Thess 5:1-6; Matt 24:42-44.)

Day 3

7. Explain the meaning of the word "Armageddon" and the historical significance of the place. Also, what is the symbolic meaning for John (16:16)? (See Judg 5:12-13, 19-20; 2 Kgs 23:29-30.)

8. Why would John's readers have recognized that "the great harlot" stood for Rome (17:1)?

9. John alerts readers to pay special attention to what follows (17:9). How does God get your attention?

Day 4

10. What do we learn about God's sovereignty in 17:9-14? (See 1 Tim 6:13-16.)

11. Recall and describe a time you have seen evil turn on itself and self-destruct (17:17)?

12. Reflect on the habitual thought patterns and behaviors that serve to remind you that you are "with the Lamb . . . called, chosen, and faithful" (17:14).

Day 5

13. Identify the characteristics of Babylon in 18:1-3.

14. As a whole, chapters 17 and 18 highlight Rome's evil ways. In what ways could the label "Babylon" be applied to our civilization today?

15. Suggest some spiritual practices that help modern-day Christians "depart" from Babylon (18:4). (See Num 16:26; Rom 12:2; Eph 5:1-5; Phil 4:8-9.)

Day 6

16. How do you feel about the vengeance that appears in 18:6-8 and in other biblical passages? (See Isa 34:8; Jer 50:15; Nah 1:2.)

17. Why are the merchants of the earth mourning (18:11-17)? (See Ezek 26:16-17; 27:12-22, 31-36.)

18. Comment on this quote from 1 Timothy 6:10: "the love of money is the root of all evils." (See Matt 6:24.)

Revelation 19–22

NCBC-NT VOLUME 12, PAGES 80–94

Day 1

1. Choose one word, phrase, or passage from last week's lesson that made you stop and think. Write about it.

2. Both the bride and the wedding day of the Lamb are used as metaphors (19:7-8). What do they symbolize? (See 21:2; Matt 7:11; 22:1-14; 25:1-13.)

3. What is the meaning of the word "Alleluia" (19:1, 3, 4, 6)? (See Ps 19:6; 150.)

Day 2

4. John is told to worship God, not the angel (19:10). Discuss the need for this warning.

5. The rider (the risen Christ) is called "Faithful and True,""the Word of God," and "King of kings and Lord of lords" (19:11-16; 3:14). Decide which of these titles leads you most comfortably into prayer and tell why.

6. As he does often in Revelation, John borrows from apocalyptic literature in Ezekiel to describe "God's great feast." Contrast Ezekiel 39:17-20 with the wedding feast in 19:17-18.

Day 3

7. Review the three purposes of apocalyptic literature from lesson one. How does knowing John's purpose affect the way you view the violence in chapter 19? (See esp. 19:15-20 and commentary introduction, page 11.)

8. What does a thousand years represent (20:1-6)? (See 12:10-12.)

9. Imagine that one of your loved ones was martyred for the faith. How would John's message in 20:4-6 help you?

Day 4

10. More destruction by the devil occurs in 20:7-10.

    a) Discuss the source of John's reference to Gog, the King, and Magog. (See Ezek 38:1–39:20.)

    b) What is John trying to say to his readers?

11. What did first century Jews believe about the resurrection of the dead (20:12-13)? (See Dan 7:10.)

12. "The dead were judged according to their deeds" (20:13). By which attitudes, behaviors, and actions do you hope to be judged?

Day 5

13. List traditional images that John borrows from Hebrew (Old Testament) Scriptures as he describes the new Jerusalem (21:9-21). (See Isa 25:7-8; 49:18; Ezek 37:26-27.)

14. Name the characteristics (and their significance) of the "new Jerusalem" (21:9-21). (See Exod 28:17-21; 1 Kgs 6:20; Ezek 41:21.)

15. There is no need for a temple in the new Jerusalem. Explain why (21:22-24).

Day 6

16. a) What is the most likely message of 22:11?

    b) What circumstances have made it hardest for you to "still be holy"?

17. a) How well are you able to identify spiritual thirst in yourself (22:17)?

    b) Provide examples of "life-giving water" in your own life (21:6).

18. How has this study helped you prepare for the coming of the Lord? And how can it help you work to bring about God's kingdom here and now?

NOTES

ABBREVIATIONS

Books of the Bible

Gen—Genesis
Exod—Exodus
Lev—Leviticus
Num—Numbers
Deut—Deuteronomy
Josh—Joshua
Judg—Judges
Ruth—Ruth
1 Sam—1 Samuel
2 Sam—2 Samuel
1 Kgs—1 Kings
2 Kgs—2 Kings
1 Chr—1 Chronicles
2 Chr—2 Chronicles
Ezra—Ezra
Neh—Nehemiah
Tob—Tobit
Jdt—Judith
Esth—Esther
1 Macc—1 Maccabees
2 Macc—2 Maccabees
Job—Job
Ps(s)—Psalm(s)
Prov—Proverbs
Eccl—Ecclesiastes
Song—Song of Songs
Wis—Wisdom
Sir—Sirach
Isa—Isaiah
Jer—Jeremiah
Lam—Lamentations
Bar—Baruch
Ezek—Ezekiel
Dan—Daniel
Hos—Hosea
Joel—Joel
Amos—Amos

Obad—Obadiah
Jonah—Jonah
Mic—Micah
Nah—Nahum
Hab—Habakkuk
Zeph—Zephaniah
Hag—Haggai
Zech—Zechariah
Mal—Malachi
Matt—Matthew
Mark—Mark
Luke—Luke
John—John
Acts—Acts
Rom—Romans
1 Cor—1 Corinthians
2 Cor—2 Corinthians
Gal—Galatians
Eph—Ephesians
Phil—Philippians
Col—Colossians
1 Thess—1 Thessalonians
2 Thess—2 Thessalonians
1 Tim—1 Timothy
2 Tim—2 Timothy
Titus—Titus
Phlm—Philemon
Heb—Hebrews
Jas—James
1 Pet—1 Peter
2 Pet—2 Peter
1 John—1 John
2 John—2 John
3 John—3 John
Jude—Jude
Rev—Revelation